How Successful People Think Smart

7 Ways YOU Can
Develop Their Mind Power

By
Dr. Jill Ammon-Wexler

Soft Cover Edition
Published August 2014

Dr. Jill Ammon-Wexler

ISBN-10:0991037928
ISBN-13:978-0-9910379-2-6

Softcover Edition
Published by
Quantum Self Group, Inc.
217 Cedar Street #268,
Sandpoint, Idaho 83864 USA

CONTENTS

Dr. Jill Ammon-Wexler

INSIDE THIS BOOK

Recent research of healthy brains reminds us that merely thinking about something changes your brain. This book was created to deliver life-changing information in an easily understood, non complex manner.

At this very moment – as you read these words – your brain is making instant physical changes. Brand new neural connections are being created and, at the same time, old neural connections are being modified or eliminated.

You're about to discover how the brains of winner's are different, and exactly *why* these differences create huge advantages. THE IMPORTANT POINT IS THIS: These differences are *not* present at birth – they are *learned!*

Obviously just knowing about these brain-based differences is not enough, so this book provides exercises and insights to guide you in developing the same advantages in your own brain.

One last point: I am a doctor of psychology with a 45-year speciality in how our brains create behavior and govern our potential. My personal mission is to make this information understandable and useful to those who want to make their lives and businesses more successful and a better place to be.

There's nothing you'll have to struggle to understand in this book. Each winner's advantage is tied to how they *taught* their brain to function. Clear insights and exercises then guide you in developing your own winner's brain power.

Enjoy the journey ... *and* your enhanced brain power!

Dr. Jill Ammon-Wexler

WHERE IT ALL STARTS

People who are successful in their personal and business lives all share one common secret – they've learned to use their brain in some very special ways. The result? A massive increase in personal power, and the resulting ability to achieve their dreams and goals while others fall by the wayside discouraged.

Let's face it – your brain is your ultimate success tool. Literally everything you think, dream, say and do all starts in the same place – your amazing 3-pound brain.

All creativity, personal power, and success start there. And YOU alone make the choice to develop, or overlook, your brain's awesome potential.

Your brain is far more than the simple stimulus-response machine it was once thought to be. It's actually the most dynamic, changeable organ of your entire body. In just the past few years, scientists have found that your brain *constantly* alters itself to adapt to your thoughts, actions and circumstances.

Dr. Jill Ammon-Wexler

Meet the Winner's Brain

The brain of a winner is different from the brain of an average person. But winners were <u>not</u> necessarily born hardwired with high performance brains. Our brain changes and develops according to what we choose to do with its potential.

The differences in the winner's brain are the result of a brain characteristic scientists call "neuroplasticity." What is neuroplasticity? Today's high tech brain studies have established that every time we feel an emotion, take an action, or even think a thought, our brain responds by immediately changing.

You can literally build a more efficient and capable brain by taking control of this process.

Winner's brains have several special characteristics you'll discover in these pages, including a seemingly endless ability to sustain an effort, outrageous creativity, and an exceptional ability to maintain motivation and focus on goal-directed behavior.

As a result winners think and act far more efficiently and effectively than ordinary people. But remember this -- these traits are *learned*, not born!

Brain Anatomy

When asked to visualize their brains most people picture a grey mass that somehow allows them to remember and think. This book is *not* a course on brain function and anatomy. Still, it is often very helpful to begin to think of your brain in terms of its sophisticated physical structure and functions.

Several areas of the brain are known to be especially critical to the high performance winner's brain, ranging from the cortex down to the brain stem.

The first time such an area is mentioned I will explain a little bit about it. In the meantime, here is a simplified function-related picture of your brain that you can refer back to:

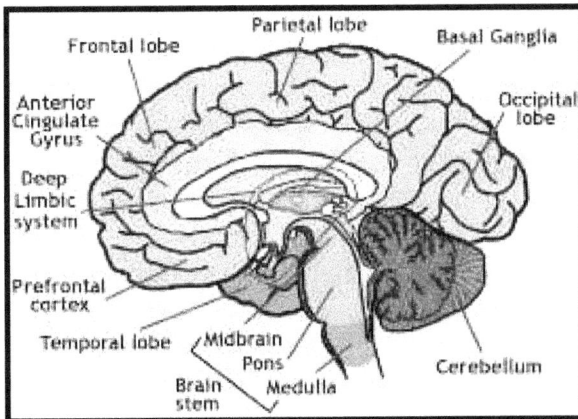

So this takes us to a question: Just what makes a winner's brain so different?

Dr. Jill Ammon-Wexler

The Winner's Brain

Getting what you want in life actually has very *little* to do with your education, your IQ, your financial situation, who you know or what your parents do. It has virtually everything to do with what's happening in your brain and how you either react, or respond, to it.

It's important to truly recognize that your brain is *not* a static organ. It changes with virtually every one of your thoughts, memories, emotions or actions.

You can literally TRAIN your brain to duplicate the special ways winners have developed and use their brains. This book focuses on *how* to unlock your brain's potential to help YOU achieve your dreams and goals faster.

The 7 very specific things that make winner's brains different are:

1. **A Functional Balance.** Winners have fully developed the ability to *simultaneously* use *both* sides of their brain ... while ordinary people have primarily one side or the other in charge of their thinking and responses.

2. **Refined Focus**. Winners have a refined ability to focus on a problem or activity in spite of what's going on around them. They have

also developed the extremely valuable ability to single-task, rather than multi-task.

3. **Steady Motivation.** For most people their motivation comes and goes. Winners, on the other hand, have discovered ways to prime their brain to push right through the occasional boring tasks and bumps in the road that stop ordinary people in their tracks.

4. **Flexible Thinking.** Winners actively stretch their brains in ways that allow them to easily identify new and unique answers to challenges.

5. **Unusual Creativity.** Winners tend to use their creative muscles in a very special way to create more "Aaha" breakthroughs, creative insights and promising new solutions.

6. **Unstoppable Resilience**. Knock a winner to the ground and they'll be back on their feet even more determined. They know that any so-called "failure" simply eliminates one possible approach to a question or challenge that does not work. *This is a learned skill.*

7. **Future Orientation**. Winners look to the future and not the past.

How have winners developed all of these unique brain powers? This all starts with one's level of awareness. Winners have developed a *refined self-*

awareness that makes them more conscious of what's going on around them, including the responses of others to their plans and actions.

The following pages provide tips and strategies to help YOU expand your own awareness and use it to build a winner's brain power.

STRATEGY 1. A BALANCED BRAIN

One of the reasons winners are so successful is that they have learned to simultaneously use *both* sides of their cortex. Ordinary people, on the other hand, usually have an emphasis on only one side of their cortex – the creative right side, or the analytical left side.

Some Useful Terms

Your *cerebral cortex*, the outermost covering of your brain, is often referred to as your "grey matter." It has four lobes important to your brain's thinking power, and enables you to perceive and interact with the outside world.

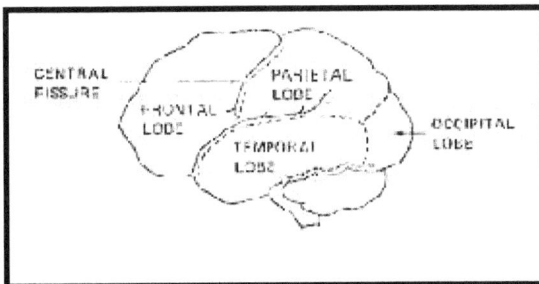

Packed inside your cerebral cortex are two types of cells: (1) The *neurons* that support your brain's signal-processing network.

Your neurons (often referred to as "brain cells") process and transmit information using a combination of electrical and chemical signals, and then connect to each other create *neural networks.*

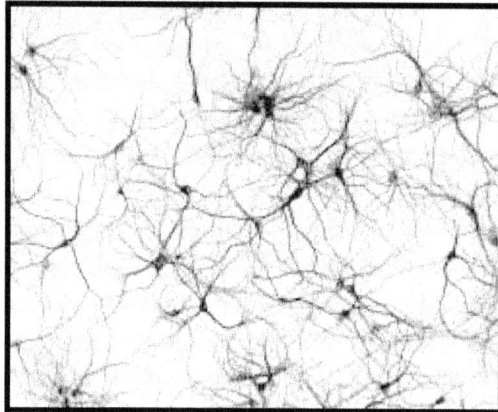

A typical neural network

(2) Your brain's *glial cells,* on the other hand, combine to create the "highways" that establish communication among your different cortical regions and the remainder of your body's nervous system.

Your Two-Sided Cortex

Your cortex is divided into two halves – the right hemisphere and the left hemisphere. The two sides provide different functions. The right is basically structured to provide more creative and flexible visual and spatial processing.

The left side of your cortex is far more structured, more analytical, and focused on language and symbols.

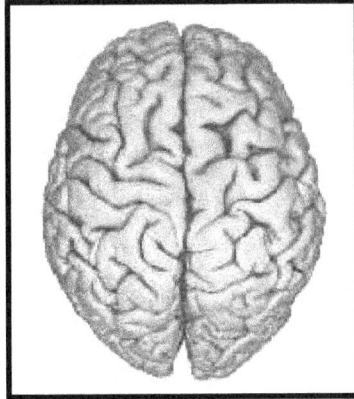

The Corpus Callosum

A very thick band of glial cells in between the two sides of the cortex, the *corpus callosum,* bridges the deep groove between the hemispheres and passes information between the two sides.

Whole Brain Thinking

Winners have developed their brains to go far beyond the common "one-sided" thinking of most people. They use both hemispheres *simultaneously* to perform whole brain thinking.

This may be one "secret key" to exceptional genius like that of Leonardo da Vinci, whose capabilities spanned and embraced both science and art.

Whole Brain Thinking Tips

Whole brain thinking uses both sides of the cortex simultaneously. It is a *learned,* brain-based art! The most effective ways to develop whole brain thinking are engineered brainwave training, or a combination of mental and physical exercises designed to improve your concentration, alertness and memory.

Developing both sides of your brain greatly boosts both your powers of perception and your creative imagination. If you are in business, whole brain thinking will greatly expand your entrepreneurial potential. If you are in the creative arts, it will support more creative analysis of your medium.

Three non-technical and easy ways to stimulate both sides of your brain include: (1) Creating and using mind maps, (2) the cross crawl exercise, and (3) a solution-seeking method that I call the "alternate occupation" method. All of these simply methods will create new connections between your cerebral hemispheres via the corpus callosum.

Mind Mapping helps your brain streamline thoughts and develop new associations and links between logic and creative ideas. It helps improve your imagination and creativity. At the same time it encourages integration between the two sides of your brain because it involves both logic and creativity.

Note: A list of several FREE mind mapping software applications is included in the Appendix of the book.

Cross Crawls is a seated physical exercise that simply involves touching your right elbow to your left knee, and alternately the left elbow to the right knee about 25 times within a period of 2 minutes. This improves your cross hemispheric communication via your brain's motor center and the corpus callosum. It also pumps a refreshing new supply of oxygen into your brain!

The "Alternate Occupation" is a playful method I have developed that stimulates whole brain thinking when you're seeking a new answer to a question or problem. Suppose you are an engineer and tend to be left-brain dominant and highly analytical. You are trying to solve a design problem, but so far are not satisfied with your potential solutions.

You could use the alternate occupation method to ask yourself how a right-brain dominant garden designer would approach the project ... or how an artist would "see" the solution. This method will often provide some amazing insights and breakthroughs.

Dr. Jill Ammon-Wexler

Note: If you're looking for a faster "high tech" whole brain solution, some excellent engineered brainwave training resources are listed in the Appendix.

STRATEGY 2. THE POWER OF FOCUS

Often today we find ourselves literally surrounded by distractions. A study of office workers reported that the average office worker switches tasks every three or four minutes. It can then take them up to 30 minutes to refocus on their original task.

This is the loss of efficiency that comes with multi-tasking. In this chapter you'll learn some ways to build the power of focus required to single-task like a winner.

How Winners Focus

The winner's brain allows them to focus on a desired task *regardless* of what's going on around them. They have developed a refined ability to single-task, rather than multi-task. Plus they have taught themselves to immediately adjust the intensity of their focus to best fit the job at hand.

Winners have literally trained their brains to switch between seeing the "forest" or a single "tree." They can switch rapidly between their "big picture" and "zoom" lenses because they have trained their brains to work with a structure in the brain's frontal lobe called the *anterior cingulated cortex*, or ACC. This enables the winner to easily switch focus and boost their attention to what's most important for the task at hand – an outrageously valuable skill.

Building your power of attention and concentration actually changes the physical structure and function of your brain – something you too can learn.

Turn on your Zoom Lens

When you realize you've lost your focus, it's time to reorient your brain. One very effective way to recover from mind wandering is to momentarily zoom in on your immediate environment.

Try this: What sounds do you hear? What is the texture of your clothing against your arms? What do you smell? Pay attention to as much detail as possible and really pull a sharp zoom focus into the *present moment*.

Next turn this same level of focus onto the task you're facing. (1) Remind yourself of your goal for this task and *why* it is important. (2) If possible eliminate distractions like email or cell phones.

(3) Then really *notice* what you're working on. Look at the big picture and *then* dig down into the smaller details.

If you compare this to the ability to "see the forest OR the trees" ... this is drilling down to the individual tree level.

What you're doing is refining your ability to distribute your brain's resources. You're using your ACC to fire up your *prefrontal cortex,* a brain structure that helps you control your "attentional narrow" (zoom) focus.

The more effort you put into training your brain to pay attention and drill down to fine details, the greater power of focus you'll develop.

 **Focus on the Big Picture**

The other end of focus is *wide* focus – seeing "the overall forest rather than an individual tree." Winners use this type of focus to get an overview and connect the individual parts of their goal plan.

This type of focus gently activates the big *visual cortex* in the back of your head. You "see" the big picture, putting less emphasis on each smaller detail.

The key to wide focus is relaxation. Letting go of active analysis lets your brain reflect. This turns on the parts of the brain that are active when you daydream or allow your mind to "wander."

When you choose to do this you are activating your *medial prefrontal cortex* that is tied to increased creativity and self expression. It's the amazing part of your brain that lights up when you get an exciting new insight.

One of the best ways to build this capability is meditation, although you can also build this skill using engineered brainwave training audios and focus training programs.

STRATEGY 3. UNSTOPPABLE MOTIVATION

For most people, motivation seems to just come and go, and their true personal potential lies largely dormant and untapped. This will remain so unless something changes. This is where the importance of refining your motivation enters the picture.

There are many steps associated with pursuing a goal, but one of the most important is learning to build and *maintain* your motivation.

Motivation in the Winner's Brain

Most winners are known for their unstoppable drive and persistence. So how do they manage to maintain motivation through the more boring and often slower parts of pursuing a goal?

Like all other aspects of being a winner, this too relates directly to *how* they have *learned* to use their brains.

Winners have taught themselves to view the necessary "mundane" goal activities in terms of the positive results they can produce.

This is an activity of the *amygdale* and your brain's *limbic system* emotional center, and underscores the important role that emotional evaluations play in motivation.

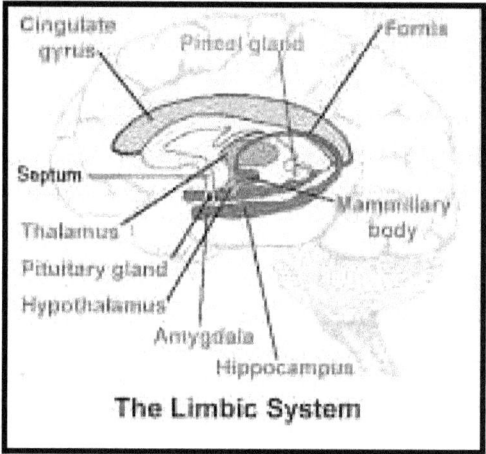

The Limbic System

How you emotionally evaluate any task or challenge has amazing power. A negative evaluation is outright de-motivating, while a positive evaluation builds motivation.

Winners remind themselves of the big picture connected to their goal, and view completion of each ordinary task as bringing them one step closer to that desired positive final outcome.

"Feel Good" Brain Juices

To develop a winner's level of motivation it is important to encourage yourself to feel inspired by completing the small everyday "mundane" tasks that take you toward your goal. The more inspiration you can build about completing these tasks, the faster you'll reach your desired goals.

Reward yourself for completing little tasks. Why is this important? The uplifting burst of warm positive energy you feel when you pat yourself on the back for completing a task is your brain in action.

You have then triggered an important part of your brain that's responsible for regulating motivation – the *ventral tegmental* area of your midbrain. This causes your brain to release dopamine – a powerful natural "feel good" biochemical.

Goal Motivation Tip

If you are having some trouble staying focused and motivated on a long term goal, there's an easy solution: Just take steps to analyze and break your goal down into a series of smaller sub goals – each of which will produce a *clearly recognizable outcome.*

Try to keep your sub-goals short – a task that can be accomplished in the period of a week or 10 days. Then reward yourself when you accomplish that task and go on to the next.

Pacing yourself in this way feeds your motivation as your brain pumps out "feel good" dopamine. This is why there is no more rewarding "pat on the back" then the one you give yourself.

Boost your Dopamine Levels

Are you missing a motivational spark in your life? The answer could be your brain chemistry. We all need good levels of the brain's neurotransmitter dopamine in order to feel motivated, focused, enthusiastic and energized.

When dopamine levels are low your concentration may be poor and you'll struggle to stay motivated. Following are some ways to rapidly increase your dopamine level:

Eat Protein. Your body makes dopamine from tyrosine – an amino acid found in proteins like eggs, cheese, fish and turkey. Eat 20 to 30 grams of protein at each meal. Over time you will see an increase in both your motivation and your ability to concentrate.

Go Easy on Sugar. Sugar causes a short term surge in dopamine production and creates a "sugar hit" short-term boost in energy, productivity and focus. But unfortunately your brain adapts to these surges by becoming less and less sensitive to dopamine.

Take Tyrosine Supplements. Tyrosine creates a natural and sustained increase in dopamine levels by providing your brain with the basic building blocks it needs for dopamine production. L-tyrosine capsules can be purchased from most health food stores.

Eat Fish or Fish Oil. Eating omega-3 assists with dopamine production. The easiest way to increase your omega-3 intake is a high quality fish-oil capsule. Be sure it is "molecularly distilled," indicating that contaminants such as mercury and dioxin have been removed at the molecular level.

Get in the Sun. Sunshine stimulates the production of the Vitamin D tht is required for the production of dopamine.

Relax. When you're stressed your adrenal glands pump out adrenaline. This greatly depletes your dopamine levels. Incorporate short relaxation periods into your daily routine.

STRATEGY 4. FLEXIBLE THINKING

Many people today live in what's often called the "comfort zone." What is the comfort zone? It is each person's unique collection of habits they use to automatically simplify their thinking, their actions, and their lives.

The comfort zone is eating the same foods, reading the same magazines or books, driving the same way 5 days a week to work, doing the same thing every Wednesday night, and thoughtlessly following the same rituals day after day.

The comfort zone runs their life by directing their actions and thoughts along the same old well-established neural networks. No new thinking or analysis is required, and therefore no brain growth is stimulated.

In fact, most people focused on living in the comfort zone will avoid new actions and thoughts because they take too much effort (the creation of new neural networks in the brain).

Winners Stretch Their Brains

Winners absolutely do NOT, NOT live in the comfort zone. They tend to actively seek out stimulating insights, information and activities that will help them better analyze and solve challenges.

The net result is a thicker *corpus callosum* (the connection between the two sides of the cortex) plus more glial cells connecting the different parts of the brain.

Researcher Marian Diamond spent years analyzing the preserved brain of the great modern genius Albert Einstein.

What did Diamond find? Einstein's brain had *massive* highways of glial cells and was packed with an abnormal amount of neural networks.

Where did this come from? Einstein stretched his brain far beyond the comfort zone as he searched for unknown answers to the secrets of the universe.

Stretch to a Better Brain

Winners stretch into the unknown to do what Einstein did. An engineer might take up painting to better learn to develop his creative muscles. A dancer might write a book to connect more logical analysis to her creative movements.

Fluff out your hair like Einstein!

You get the picture. The most productive way to reach a goal could be taking a dramatic turn in the road. Try thinking and doing things differently. The comfort zone is useful for brushing your teeth and dressing yourself, but you don't want to waste time analyzing how to do these tasks.

When it comes to solving a problem however, move yourself out of your comfort zone. Ask impossible questions and come up with impossible answers. Get radical and explore the meaning of yourproject, or even of your life!

Build a More Flexible Brain

Optimal brain function is *not* something we're born with, nor is it accidental. Having optimal brain function is the result of how we each CHOOSE to use and care for our brain.

Get Physical. This will stretch the capacity of the capillaries in your brain. This creates better blood flow and the resulting increased oxygen in the brain. Interestingly, this also promotes the growth of new glial cells and neurons.

Drink More Water. The deficiency of only one cup of water can significantly lower your IQ.

Eat Healthy Fat. Today's low fat diets do not make your brain smarter! Fats are a major component of your brain cells. Good brain fat is found in foods like fish, nuts, coconut oil and eggs – polyunsaturated fats derived from long-chain omega-3 fatty acids.

Organic Fruits and Veggies. These are natural sources of the antioxidants that help guard from oxidative damage to your brain, and also boost synaptic communication among neurons.

Control Your Stress. A certain amount of stress is a good thing, but out of control or chronic stress is another story. Chronic and acute stress have been shown to kill your neurons (brain cells).

Walk, run, meditate, listen to brainwave audios, perform progressive relaxation, do yoga, go to the gym or beat up a pillow – but DO find a way to keep your stress under control.

Dr. Jill Ammon-Wexler

STRATEGY 5. BOOST CREATIVITY

Creative thinking is not a passive process. When you engage in a creative activity very specific parts of your brain are active, while others are shut down.

Your brain's left cerebral hemisphere is composed of neatly stacked vertical columns. This lets it clearly set apart unique mental functions, but it does *not* integrate those functions.

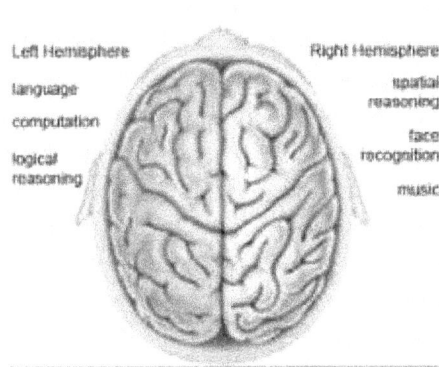

Your right cerebral hemisphere, on the other hand, has more neural connections both within itself and reaching out to the rest of the brain. It has especially strong connections to the amygdale and regions in the central and lower parts of the brain.

Creativity therefore involves not just the right-brain cortex itself, it also stimulates desirable whole brain integration with strong ties to your brain's important emotional limbic system.

Creativity in the Winner's Brain

Winners use their creative muscles to create new responses to challenges and problems. They tend to be more sensitive and responsive to sensory stimulation, and have developed unique ways of turning on their creativity.

The *frontal and temporal lobes* of the cortex generate creative ideas by working together using mutually inhibitory pathways.

Research has shown that the winner's creative drive is stronger due to a higher level of activity in the dopamine pathways in their brain's emotional center – the limbic system.

In short, winners tend to feel and express their emotions. This is why you will benefit from building your dopamine levels.

There's strong evidence that winners often slip into a deeply relaxed mental zone in which ideas come up freely. At that time a part of the brain known as the *association cortex* becomes very active and links up ideas in novel ways. Einstein was said to often spend long unbroken hours in this super creative mental state.

Turn Up Your Emotions

Because of the intimate connection between your emotions and creativity, you can see how being closed down emotionally could greatly depress your creativity.

You want to stir up the amygdale that attach emotional meaning to your thoughts, and stoke your limbic center by *openly* feeling excitement about your goals.

Do a Creative Workout

You can build a more creative brain by dedicating some time and effort to creativity "workouts:"

Explore unfamiliar topics. If you use a lot of math or calculation, sign up for a painting class and try your hand at painting.

Spend time thinking. Take some time to allow your mind to "play" with possible solutions to a problem and just see what comes up. Avoid being critical or analytical with what comes up – remember you're playing!

Pay attention. Really observe a person or an object and try describing it to yourself in unique ways.

Encourage "AaHa!" Insights

Brainwave studies indicate that during an "aaha insights" you have a very high Gamma brainwave spike 300 milliseconds *before* the answer surfaces.

This level of Gamma brainwave activity is generated as distant neurons suddenly connect to create a brand new neural network. The new insight can then enter your conscious awareness. This exciting heightened activity occurs in the temporal area of your right cortex.

What's happened is that the neurons in the temporal area of your right cortex have created long arms of communication that reach into other parts of the brain. This collects varied information that is then put together in a new way.

You *CAN* develop this winner's brain ability. Here's how:

(1) First concentrate intently on your goal or problem.

(2) Then relax deeply until you forget the problem and just let go into reverie. This condition is characterized by the high Alpha brainwaves that set the stage for the novel connections that occur during the Gamma spike.

(3) Finally, let go but do *not* go to sleep. Just allow your mind to drift around the topic at hand.

So ... the preparation for Gamma spike includes defining the problem, immersing yourself in it, and then letting go.

Dr. Jill Ammon-Wexler

STRATEGY 6. UNSTOPPABLE RESILIENCE

Our ability to deal effectively with challenges is a refined skill. It is the direct result of the saying that it is truly wise to "know thyself." What is resilience? It's the ability to CHOOSE how you will INTERPRET what's happening inside your own self and in the outside environment.

Choosing how to *interpret* what's happening is very different from automatic knee-jerk reactions to people and events.

This is a refined skill that is basically *learned*, and leads to developing a resilient winner's brain.

The Winner's Resilient Brain

Knock a winner to the ground and they'll be back on their feet even more determined. They know that any "failure" simply eliminates one possible approach to a question or challenge that does not work.

This is the key to the winner's personality trait known as "resilience."

Using resilience, wwinner's have discovered ways to prime their brain to push right through the bumps in the road that stop ordinary people in their tracks.

Alpha Breaks

Are you aware that your thoughts and moods are *real* brain states that directly impact your thinking? In terms of the goals of this book, a quick "Alpha break" provides the instant physical and mental recharge you need to create a winner's resilience.

Normally we automatically drop into Alpha brainwaves several times a day, but it's very useful to learn to do this "on command." If you meditate you have probably already developed this ability. If not, an engineered Alpha brainwave training will get you there instantly.

Not only does Alpha build brain-based resilience, short Alpha brainwave sessions have the same positive effect as a 30-minute nap.

STRATEGY 7. FUTURE ORIENTATION

Suppose you are out golfing with a friend at your favorite course. Your friend tees off with a fabulous long drive and lands right on the green.

You instantly recall the last time *you* shot for that green and ended up in the trees. Guess what then happens: Your subconscious mind instantly "gets the picture" and sends a message to your brain's motor centers to create an identical drive straight into the trees.

So ... do you think your ball will end up on the green? Unlikely! You'll probably land in the trees again.

What happened? You created a brain-based vision of your previous drive, and your subconscious mind then interpreted that vision as an "action direction."

Let's apply this to another life scenario. Suppose you have a goal of improving your financial well being. But when you plan your actions, your brain automatically focuses on memories of some related "past failures." What results can you expect when you try to create a successful outcome?

Brain Focus on Past "Failures"

Why does your brain tend to focus on related past "failures?" Your brain automatically does this because when presented with a task, it automatically turns to the strongest neural networks related to that task.

So ... since your so-called past financial failures are stored in well established neural networks, that will be the first place your subconscious thoughts will land.

Then your brain will *automatically try to* push you to take the same actions and hold the same thoughts that led to your prior *unsuccessful* results.

The interesting thing is that your brain uses this process constantly. There's actually no way to turn it off. You are constantly either creating visions of success, OR visions of failure.

Your Subconscious Guidance System

Your powerful subconscious mind makes sure that your every thought, feeling, emotion and action corresponds to your mental pictures. **As a result, your mental pictures actually serve as your subconscious guidance system.**

The way you react from moment to moment is *totally* consistent with your subconscious guidance system.

It guides you toward actions and behaviors that will manifest the dreams and goals you picture in your future (whether positive or negative).

Your daily reality is therefore a direct reflection of your vision of the future. Whatever you consciously or unconsciously focus on and project as an expectation for the future, whether positive or negative, will guide your beliefs and actions.

This is actually the *direct cause* of almost every success and every failure.

 Now you understand why any positive life change *must* begin with an improvement in your ability to look to the future and put the past behind you. You must re-program your brain!

Winners build and focus on clear visions of the future life they desire. Unsuccessful people continually build and focus on memories of what they do NOT want in their future life. It really *IS* that simple!

It's important to understand that your vision of your future is a *physical* brain reality. This is NOT just a psychological construct.

Consider the process of seeing, and how your brain processes what you visualize. A surprising 25% of your brain is actively involved in the complex process of seeing, and then interpreting, what you see.

However what your eyes actually "see" is ONLY light being reflected off the surface of something. That's it. Your eyes then convert the reflected light into electrical signals and send the signals into your brain via the optic nerve.

Your brain then analyzes these signals and uses them to create a *mental picture* of what you "saw."So when you say you see something, what you really "see" is only a mental picture that was actually assembled and created in your own brain.

That brings us to the amazing and very real power of "visualization." **Just like when you *see* something with your eyes, visualization creates very real _physical_ electrical and chemical signals in your brain.**

This explains why, in terms of the winner's brain, using mental imagery to visualize the future is just as real as the normal "seeing" process.

Build New Neural Networks

Suppose you have a dream or goal of creating the financial well being necessary to live your dream lifestyle. If you focus on a clear vision of having this future financial well being, you're actually using your brain to see yourself in the future having achieved this.

As you replay that vision you create *very real* physical neural networks in your brain to support it. The more you focus on a positive vision of your future, the stronger and more stable those physical neural networks will become.

Plus something wonderful happens IF, at the same time, you also consciously refuse to pay attention to any old negative memories.

The neural networks holding those old memories will then begin to lose the synaptic connections that glues them together. And if you refuse to give them attention long enough, they will eventually be "pruned away" just like a gardener cuts off a dead branch. This is solid modern neurological science, *not* a metaphor or imagined concept.

ALL you have read here is under your control. You <u>CAN</u> build a winner's brain. What is required is simply a decision, then taking the resulting actions!

APPENDIX

1. Special Brainwave Training Audios

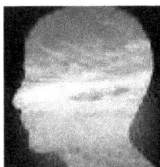 Come explore a unique collection of powerful *downloadable* brainwave training audios specially engineered by Dr. Ammon-Wexler to help your brain better create and sustain higher levels of performance=>

http://www.QuantumLeapAudios.com

2. The QUANTUM MIND Program

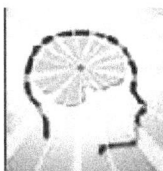 If YOU are one of those special people with a truly passionate commitment to personal development and goal achievement, go investigate the author's unique 3-month online Quantum Mind training program. Come learn more about the program (and take advantage of a substantial book buyer's discount) here=>

http://www.hotbrainz.com

3. Other Books and Programs

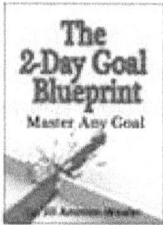

Dr. Ammon-Wexler's ebooks, books, and goal and success training programs are available here, along with many fascinating articles=>

http://www.buildmindpower.com

4. FREE Mind Mapping Software

Mind mapping involves creating a diagram that represents ideas or words. To create a mind map a keyword is placed in the center, then associated words or tasks are linked around it in a tree branch format.

The below mind mapping downloads come with built-in features to simplify this process.

Blumind – a free powerful lightweight brainstorming and mind mapping utility. It can be customized to fit the user's needs and has all the features expected in a complete mind mapping software=>

http://blumind.org/

The Brain – a freeware application for mind mapping and brainstorming. Everything needed to express your thoughts ideas in visible form. Great for business or personal purposes. The program is loaded with built-in features and is very easy to use=>

http://www.thebrain.com/c/personalbrain/?c =32&gclid=CL_T4Z2LjLYCFch7QgodElMAgQ

Edraw Mind Map – a freeware application with built-in templates and examples. Very easy to use. Features include: smart drawing guide that makes drawing easy, support for large multiple page map, themes, MA Office, and easy to share maps=>

http://www.edrawsoft.com/freemind.php

Dr. Jill Ammon-Wexler

ABOUT THE AUTHOR

Jill Ammon-Wexler is doctor of positive psychology and a pioneer brain/mind and neuropsychology researcher since 1968. She is also a life adventurer with a passion for pushing beyond her own personal limits.

During her university years she studied with amazing leaders like Fritz Perls, Virginia Satir, Soygal Rinpoche and Alan Watts. She also walked on fire, did sweat lodges, studied with shamanic elders, and become the holder of a coyote talking stick.

After receiving her Masters degree in psychology, she spent 6 months in a monastic Buddhist retreat. She then completed a PhD in psychology, became certified as a clinical hypnotherapist and clinical biofeedback provider, and began her professional career as a pioneer mind power trainer and personal transformation coach.

Over the years Dr. Jill Ammon-Wexler has provided mind power training for companies, organizations and individuals from around the world.

Information about Dr. Ammon-Wexler's other mind-expanding books and success training programs can be found at=> **http://www.BuildMindPower.com**

www.ingramcontent.com/pod-product-compliance
Lightning Source LLC
Chambersburg PA
CBHW060618030426
42337CB00018B/3114